The Beauty & Bounty
OF HURON COUNTY

TELFER WEGG • DAVID BISHOP • BONNIE SITTER

The publisher and the authors gratefully acknowledge the financial support of the Huron Heritage Fund in the production of this book. Every effort has been made to properly identify people, places and wildlife and to secure permission for the use of all images. Any errors or omissions in this regard are unintentional.

T. Wegg Photography, P.O. Box 36, Neustadt, Ontario N0G 2M0

Library and Archives Canada Cataloguing in Publication

Wegg, Telfer, 1941-, photographer
        The beauty and bounty of Huron County / Telfer Wegg,
Bonnie Sitter, David Bishop.

        ISBN 978-0-9698207-6-5 (bound)

        1. Huron (Ont. : County)–Pictorial works. 2. Huron (Ont. : County)–Aerial photographs. 3. Natural history–Ontario–Huron (County)–Pictorial works. 4. Agriculture–Ontario–Huron (County)–Pictorial works. 5. Huron (Ont. : County)–Description and travel–Pictorial works. I. Sitter, Bonnie, 1944-, photographer II. Bishop, David, 1959-, photographer III. Title.

FC3095.H87W43 2013   971.3'22050222   C2013-901744-5

Cover (TW)
Harvesting winter wheat on Mollard Line,
South Huron.

Back Cover (DB)
Snowy owl (*Nyctea scandiaca*).

Title Page (DB)
Maitland River near Wroxeter.

Facing Page (TW)
St. Brigids Dairy Farm, owned by Bill VanNes and family,
Brandon Road near Brussels.

CONTENTS

Photo (TW)
Maitland River, Gorrie.

FOREWORD

"Ontario's West Coast" – the official slogan of Huron County serves it well and confirms its fortunate position bordering Lake Huron. Both residents and visitors agree, however, that many other features of the county deserve recognition and celebration.

First and foremost, Huron is the agricultural breadbasket of Ontario, with total farm sales ranking first among all Ontario counties. Its varied industries include the world's largest salt mine, the world's leading supplier of cast exhaust manifolds and an ice-sculpture creator serving global markets. Numerous large grain elevators and agricultural supply businesses serve the farming community. The natural world is well cared for, with Hullett Provincial Wildlife Management Area adding to numerous Conservation Authority properties to complement the predominant pastoral landscapes. Finally, the towns and villages of Huron deserve recognition for providing splendid opportunities to experience the best of rural lifestyles and traditions.

Keeping these attributes in mind, it has been both a challenge and a pleasure to collaborate on this visual perspective of Huron County. Our collective hope is that it provides an insight into features unappreciated by the casual observer. Our goal will be achieved if readers gain a greater awareness of their surroundings and are inspired to venture forth to make their own discoveries.

Bonnie Sitter
David Bishop
Telfer Wegg

Please note that photographer's credits are provided by initials included with each photo caption. All photos are taken in Huron County, and all are available on request either for publication or as enlargements for framing.

Top (TW)
Historic Gorrie Mill.

Above (TW)
Soybean harvest, Creek Line.

County of Huron

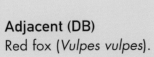

HURON
COUNTY

Produced by the County of Huron Planning and Development
Department GIS Services with data supplied under License
by Members of the Ontario Geospatial Data Exchange,
MVCA, ABCA and MNA&M.
This map is illustrative only. Do not rely on it as a precise
indicator of routes, feature locations, nor as a guide to navigation.
Copyright © Queen's Printer 2013.

Adjacent (DB)
Red fox (*Vulpes vulpes*).

HURON COUNTY
From the Air

Above Left (TW)
Steve Martin, pilot for the authors, with his airplane at Centralia Airport.

Above Right (TW)
Maitland River near Auburn.

Adjacent (TW)
Lake Huron shoreline at Poplar Beach Road south of St. Joseph.

Above (TW)
Hayter Turkey Farm (foreground) and Dashwood.

Adjacent (TW)
The Port Blake water treatment plant at the junction of Highway 21 and Highway 83. The plant treats lake water for a number of municipalities serving a total population of 350,000.

Huron Experimental Farm on Airport Road southwest of Exeter, managed by
Ridgetown College, a division of the University of Guelph. (TW)

Dungannon. (TW)

Eroded Lake Huron shoreline south of Goderich. (TW)

Facing Page (TW)
Wawanosh Lake.

Above (TW)
Harvesting soybeans near shoreline south of Goderich.

Above (TW)
Rows of green peppers in the foreground are separated by strips of rye, Bronson Line, South Huron.

Adjacent Left (BS)
Black's Point, south of Goderich.

The 730 foot freighter Algomarine arriving at Goderich to load 20,000 tonnes of Sifto salt. The tugboats Ian Mac, Debbie Lyn and Donald Bert give assistance. (TW)

Above (TW)
Londesborough

Adjacent (TW)
Londesborough Road and Maitland River
including Ball's Bridge.

Exeter. Looking east with Ironwood Golf Club in top left. (TW)

Above (TW)
Ethel and Maitland River.

Adjacent (TW)
Sand and gravel pit owned by McCann Redi-Mix Inc. on Tower Line Road west of Clinton.

Above (TW)
Grain in stooks, Ashfield-Colborne-Wawanosh Township.

Adjacent (TW)
Clinton.

Facing Page (TW)
Benmiller and Maitland River.

Bayfield. (TW)

Above (TW)
The town of Hensall lays claim to being Canada's largest inland grain terminal. The elevator complex in the upper left belongs to Hensall District Co-operative, a farmer owned agricultural service business and global marketer of grain and beans.

Above (TW)
Former VandenHeuvel farm owned by Mari VanderVeeken on Orchard Line near Goderich.

Adjacent Left (TW)
A section of Huron Experimental Farm occupies the foreground of this photo with Ondrejika Elevators in the middle distance and the 23 acre hydroponic greenhouse operated by Exeter Produce in the background. The road intersection is the junction of Airport Road and Kirkton Road.

Port Albert and the mouth of Nine Mile River. (T

Auburn, County Road 25 and the Maitland River. (TW)

Maitland River and Sharpes Creek Line north of Holmesville. (TW)

John Gaunt's Treasure Valley Crocus Farm, Belgrave Road. **(TW)**

Above (TW)
Huron Park and James T. Field Memorial Aerodrome,
formerly RCAF Station Centralia until 1967.

Adjacent (TW)
Highway 21 approaching Goderich.

Above (TW)
Zurich

Facing Page (TW)
The foreground features a traditional mixed farm owned by Raimund and Marie-Luise Eisert and their son Richard. The farm in the background is owned by Jim and Nancy Morlock. The road in the photo is Babylon Line north of Crediton.

Wawanosh Valley Conservation Area. The hedgerows provide food and shelter for wildlife. (TW)

Above (TW)
South of Grand Bend along Highway 81 toward Greenway. The farms in the foreground belong to Laurence and Jane Brown.

Adjacent (TW)
Looking east to the junction of Highway 4 and County Road 83 in north Exeter, the grading and packing plant of Exeter Produce is visible in the foreground. In the distant background are large greenhouses owned by Suntastic Hothouses Inc.

Above (TW)

Huron Ridge Acres, Bronson Line.

Adjacent Left (TW)

Post-tornado reconstruction of Goderich town square as seen in autumn of 2012.

Blyth. (TW)

Belgrave. (TW)

FLORA & FAUNA
of Huron

Above Left (DB)
Northern pintail duck (*Anus acuta*).

Above Right (BS)
Red trillium (*Trillium erectum*).

Facing Page (DB)
Great white egrets (*Camerodius albus*), Hullett Provincial Wildlife Management Area.

Beaver (*Castor canadensis*), Maitland River. **(DB)**

Belted kingfisher (*Megaceryle alcyon*), Hullett
Provincial Wildlife Management Area. **(DB)**

Red foxes (*Vulpes fulva*) near Brussels. **(DB)**

Velvet shank fungus (*Flammulina velutipes*). **(BS)**

Above (BS)
Holes made by pileated woodpecker (*Dryocopus pileatus*) in search of insects.

Facing Page (DB)
Sandhill cranes (*Grus canadensis*) near Wroxeter.

"Photo Finish." Mature (left) and immature (right) bald eagles (*Haliaeetus leucocephalus*). (DB)

Above (BS)
Autumn leaves in Ausable River.

Adjacent (DB)
Rough-legged hawk (*Buteo lagopus*).

Raccoon (*Procyon lotor*). (DB)

Rainbow trout (*Oncorhynchus mykiss*) on spawning runs, Bluevale Dam. **(DB)**

Above (DB)
White-tailed deer (*Odocoileus virginianus*) near St. Helens.

Adjacent Left (BS)
Eastern bluebirds (*Sialia sialis*).

Facing Page (BS)
Painted turtles (*Chrysemys picta marginata*), Wawanosh Lake.

Above (DB)
Great white egret (*Casmerodius albus*) near Jamestown.

Adjacent Right (DB)
Merlin (*Falco columbarius*) leaving nest at Trivitt Anglican Church, Exeter.

Facing Page (DB)
White squirrel (*Albus sciurus*). Many communities in Huron County have them, but Exeter is considered the home of the white squirrel.

Above (DB)
Snowy owl (*Nyctea scandiaca*).

Adjacent Left (DB)
Great blue heron (*Ardea herodias*).

Facing Page (BS)
American toad (*Bufo terrestris*) sitting in water lily.

Above (DB)
Ferns, Wawanosh Valley Conservation Area.

Adjacent (DB)
Common merganser (*Mergus merganser*), Maitland River.

Facing Page (DB)
Ring-necked pheasant (*Phasianus colchicus*) near Zurich.

All Photos (DB)
Bald eagles
(Haliaeetus leucocephalus)

Mink (*Mustela vison*). (DB)

Snowy owl (*Nyctea scandiaca*) with captured mouse. (DB)

Cardinal (*Richmondena cardinalis*). **(DB)**

Above (BS)
Canada geese (*Branta canadensis*).

Adjacent Right (DB)
White-tailed deer buck (*Odocoileus virginianus*) in velvet.

Above (BS)
Lacquered bracket fungus (*Ganoderma lucidum*).

Facing Page (DB)
Great blue heron (*Ardea herodias*) flying over Maitland River near Brussels.

Tundra swans (*Cygnus columbianus*), Hullett Provincial Wildlife Management Area. (DB)

Above (DB)
Tundra swans (*Cygnus columbianus*).

Adjacent (DB)
Osprey (*Pandion haliaetus*) carrying a fish.

HURON COUNTY
an Agricultural Powerhouse

Above Left (BS)
Harvesting haylage, Parr Line near Kippen.

Above Right (BS)
Hayfield Jerseys Inc. of Tipperary Line in Central Huron is a farm owned by John and Anna Brand and family; they milk 100 purebred Jersey cows.

Facing Page (TW)
T.J. Klopp of Cedar Villa Angus Farms near Zurich harvesting winter wheat on Mollard Line south of Grand Bend.

Dairy goats, Gordon's Goat Dairy near Wroxeter. (TW)

Grain corn harvest, McNaught Line near Ethel. (TW)

Above (BS). Beatrice Mendez, a worker from El Salvador, on the Exeter Produce grading line.

Exeter Produce, established in 1951, is a third generation Veri family-operated fresh produce grower and distributor delivering to markets in Canada, USA and the Caribbean. They farm 3,000 acres in the Exeter area including 800 acres of rutabagas, 600 acres of green beans, 200 acres of cabbage and 150 acres of peppers. In addition, they operate a 23 acre greenhouse producing bell peppers. In season, over 200 workers from Mexico and Jamaica help to grow, irrigate and harvest these vegetables. Without the foreign workers, it would be impossible to overcome critical seasonal deadlines. These next few pages pay testament to this industry.

Hoeing green and yellow beans near Exeter. (TW)

Above (TW)
Pepper harvest with Mexican workers, Ausable Line, South Huron.

Adjacent (TW)
Grading green beans, Exeter Produce.

Facing Page (TW)
Exeter Produce greenhouse, Airport Road, South Huron. Hydroponically grown yellow, orange and red peppers are produced year round in this 23 acre greenhouse.

Above (BS)
These domestic geese out for a winter walk are Emdens, except for one Toulouse in the middle.

Adjacent Right (BS)
Suffolk (black-faced) and Dorset (white-faced) sheep, Airport Road.

Facing Page (TW)
Ondrejika Elevators, Kirkton Road is a privately-owned grain elevator in South Huron tracing its roots to 1981. Commodities handled include corn, soybeans and wheat.

Above (BS)
Paul Van Dorp making cheese at Blyth Cheese Farm on Allboro Road. Milk from both sheep and goats is used to make a variety of artisan cheeses.

Adjacent Left (BS)
Kayla Beyerlein O'Brien surveying Bayfield Berry Farm display at Exeter market.

Fresh fruit for sale at a farmers' market. (BS)

Above (TW)
Darren Regier of Regier Farms, Goshen Line, spreading manure with a 40-tonne capacity spreader in a field beside Zurich-Hensall Road.

Adjacent (BS)
Rick and Rusty Schilbe harvesting watermelons on Orchard Line near Bayfield.

Facing Page (DB)
"Beauty Pageant." Beef cattle, North Huron.

Above (TW)

Harvesting winter wheat, Highway 84 near Zurich, with Gary Love in the front combine and Grant Love in the rear combine on the farm of Gary and Kim Love.

Adjacent (TW)

Kimberly Hendrick operating combine harvesting winter wheat beside Highway 21 north of Port Blake.

Stooked grain on Huron County Road 7 at McIntosh Line. **(TW)**

Above (BS).
Asparagus.

Adjacent Right (BS)
Friedhelm Hoffmann, General Operating Manager for Exeter Produce and Storage and Veri Hydroponics Inc.

Facing Page (TW)
M. Groot (left) and K. Weber (right) milking Holsteins on Welldale Farm, Ausable Line, South Huron. The farm is owned by Franz and Catherine Weber.

Above (TW)
Ron O'Brien no-till seeding soybeans in wheat stubble, Ausable Line, South Huron.

Adjacent Far Right (TW)
T.J. Klopp operating his combine during winter wheat harvest, South Huron.

Adjacent Right (TW)
Soybeans early in the growing season, Moncrieff Road near Walton

Facing Page (TW)
Harvesting green beans for the fresh market, Ausable Line.

OUT & ABOUT
in Huron County

Above Left (TW)
Orange Hill Road.

Above Right (BS)
Stained glass window, Trivitt Memorial Anglican Church, Exeter.

Facing Page (BS)
Icicles on footbridge over Ausable River, Exeter.

Shadow of historic Ball's Bridge on the frozen surface of the Maitland River. (BS)

A Huron County sunrise. **(DB)**

Above (DB)
Bull riding at Exeter Rodeo.

Facing Page (TW)
The Menesetung Bridge in Goderich was once a rail line carrying freight high over the Maitland River to the port at Goderich until the closure of the line in 1988. Concerned citizens came forward with funds to save the structure and preserve it as a scenic pedestrian crossing that became part of the Tiger Dunlop Heritage Trail. Names of donors are displayed on the bridge.

Above (TW)
Maitland River at Wroxeter.

Adjacent (DB)
Bill VanNes out with his team near Ethel.

Facing Page (BS)
The glory of autumn on the MacNaughton-Morrison Trail, Exeter.

Hoarfrost. (BS)

Facing Page (BS). Thin needles of larch turn golden in late autumn, Huron-Bruce Road.

Above (TW). Clinton Town Hall, built in 1880.

Adjacent Left (TW)
The Cardno Block in Seaforth was built in the Second Empire style in 1877. The distinctive clock tower with its mansard roof extends 68 feet above Main Street.

The Stevenson Tract ski trail is entered from Clyde Line and follows a ridge overlooking the Maitland River. (BS)

Orange Hill Road. (TW)

Above (TW)
Threshing demonstration at the Huron Pioneer Thresher and Hobby Association event held annually in Blyth.

Adjacent (TW)
Horses, Huron Road 7 near Belmore Line.

Above (TW)
McIntosh Line at corner of Huron Road 7.

Adjacent (DB)
"After the Storm" near Brussels.

Facing Page (TW)
Logan's Mill in Brussels was built in 1911 on the rubble stone foundation of an older mill dating from 1871.

Above (TW)
Wingham Town Hall.

Adjacent Right (BS)
"Snow pillows." Saratoga Swamp.

Facing Page (TW)
Limekiln Line south of Auburn.

Above (BS)
Crocus bulbs grown commercially, Treasure Valley Crocus Farm, Belgrave Road.

Facing Page (DB)
Frosty sunrise near Brussels.

Above (BS)
Beef cattle near Belgrave on an autumn morning.

Adjacent (TW)
Huron County Museum, Goderich, is an historic building that was originally the old Central School, erected in 1856. The property was first opened as a museum in 1951.

Facing Page (BS)
This Huron County landmark, an American elm, is located on Highway 4 north of Kippen. In 2011 the Ontario Ministry of Transport decided the tree needed to be removed because of its proximity to the highway. A protest was mounted and the healthy, mature tree was saved.

Historic schoolhouse, Kintail. (TW)

Above (TW)

Ball's Bridge, Little Lakes Road east of Benmiller. Historians view this as one of the finest bridges of its type in Canada and truly an historic landmark. It is properly described as a "twin span pin-connected Pratt through truss" bridge. Pin-connected truss bridges are very rare in Ontario and multi-span examples are rare anywhere. Metal bridges did not replace wooden structures until the 1870s, with early ones being of the 'bowstring' design. The stronger and more easily designed Pratt truss bridges appeared a decade later. The 1882 construction date of Ball's bridge mark it as one of the earliest of its type. Historical significance aside, it also has an aesthetic appeal missing in modern structures.

Interesting erosion feature in Paleozoic limestone, Maitland River near Holmesville. (BS)

Above (TW).
The Van Egmond House, Egmondville was built about 1846 by the son of Colonel Anthony Van Egmond, a leader of rebel forces in the Ontario Rebellion of 1837. Its sturdy proportions are typical of the local Canadian interpretation of the Georgian style of the era.

Adjacent (TW)
Lakelet Lake north of Fordwich.

Above (BS)
Our Lady of Mount Carmel Church, South Huron. The community of Mount Carmel was founded in the 1830s by Irish settlers who had originally homesteaded in the Pickering, Ontario area. The first small frame church was erected east of the present site in the 1840s, with the present imposing structure completed in 1888 using bricks from nearby Crediton.

Facing Page (TW)
Bluevale Mill, built in 1909 on the Little Maitland River.

Above (BS)
Sunset at the Exeter lagoon, Airport Road.

Adjacent (TW)
Auburn-Goderich rail trail, a 12 km trail connecting to the Menesetung Bridge in Goderich.

Facing Page (BS)
Tree line at edge of Lobb's Bush off Maitland Line north-east of Holmesville.

Huron Ridge Acres, Bronson Line. **(TW)**

Action at Auburn Motocross. (DB)

Above (TW)
Dashwood Mill, dating from the mid 1860s when the community was known as Friedsburg.

Adjacent Right (DB)
Wawanosh River Trail, Wawanosh Valley Conservation Area.

Facing Page (TW)
Bayfield.

Above (BS)
Lake Huron shoreline south of Bayfield.

Facing Page (TW)
The Little Inn, Bayfield. This landmark on Bayfield's main street was built in the 1830s as a stagecoach stop on the Sarnia to Goderich line. It is Ontario's longest continually operated inn. The present day bar was, in fact, the waiting room for the coach stop. Today the Little Inn is known for elegant accommodation and fine dining and has been designated a heritage site.

Above (TW)
Orange Hill Road east of Wingham.

Adjacent Left (TW)
Misty dawn alongside Toll Gate Road near Lakelet.

Facing Page (TW)
Sunset along the Goderich to Stratford railway line as viewed from level crossing at Kinburn Line.

ABOUT THE PHOTOGRAPHERS

Bonnie Hogarth Sitter's great-grandfather, Septimus Hogarth, settled in Stephen Township in 1849 and she is the fourth generation of the Hogarth family to appreciate the beauty and the bounty of Huron County. She lived for 20 years in Deep River, Ontario before returning to her birthplace in Exeter. Since retiring, after more than 40 years in the travel industry, she has become interested in photography and spends time exploring Huron County with her husband Conrad and with friends.

A passion for cross-country skiing and snowshoeing has led to winter becoming Bonnie's favourite time for photography. Her love of trees and all things in the natural world are evident in her photography.

David Bishop is a resident of Brussels in Huron County. Inspired by Huron's abundance of open spaces, woodlands and waterways, he was inspired to take up photography in a serious way in 2007. He came to realize that his greatest challenge was capturing dynamic images of wild birds and animals, caught in a brief few seconds of action and excitement. Using his camera to record these special moments gave him a great sense of accomplishment. Navigating a winter trail on snowshoes or crouching for hours in a well-hidden blind became his home away from home. Patiently searching for the "perfect light" on such excursions provided the magical moments and sense of wonder revealed in his images. His dramatic landscapes and images of nature offer a compelling look into Huron County seldom seen by the casual observer.

Telfer Wegg was raised on a York County dairy farm and has a degree in agriculture from the University of Guelph. He has been a resident of Neustadt in Grey County since 1969 and operates a stock photography business specializing in outdoor, travel and agricultural photography. More of his work can be viewed on his website, www.weggphotos.com.

Documenting the tranquil landscapes and the family farms of Ontario is one of Telfer's continuing goals. His farm background and education give him a respect for the traditions of rural life and an eye for the light and texture which creates compelling outdoor compositions. He feels fortunate to reside in Mid-Western Ontario, which remains one of the best areas to experience and photograph the rural scene.